Bible reflections
for older people

BRF
Ministries

BRF Ministries

15 The Chambers, Vineyard
Abingdon OX14 3FE
+44 (0)1865 319700 | **brf.org.uk**

Bible Reading Fellowship is a charity (233280)
and company limited by guarantee (301324)
registered in England and Wales

EU Authorised Representative: Easy Access System Europe –
Mustamäe tee 50, 10621 Tallinn, Estonia, gpsr.requests@easproject.com

ISBN 978 1 80039 366 0

Cover image: Osaze Cuomo / Alamy Stock Photo

Acknowledgements
Scripture quotations marked with the following abbreviations are taken from the version shown. Where no abbreviation is given, the quotation is taken from the same version as the headline reference. NIV: The Holy Bible, New International Version, Anglicised edition, copyright © 1979, 1984, 2011 by Biblica. Used by permission of Hodder & Stoughton Publishers, a Hachette UK company. All rights reserved. 'NIV' is a registered trademark of Biblica. UK trademark number 1448790. ESV: The Holy Bible, English Standard Version, published by HarperCollins Publishers, © 2001 Crossway Bibles, a division of Good News Publishers. Used by permission. All rights reserved. NRSV: the New Revised Standard Version Updated Edition. Copyright © 2021 National Council of Churches of Christ in the United States of America. Used by permission. All rights reserved worldwide.

Every effort has been made to trace and contact copyright owners for material used in this resource. We apologize for any inadvertent omissions or errors, and would ask those concerned to contact us so that full acknowledgement can be made in the future.

A catalogue record for this book is available from the British Library

Printed and bound in the UK by Zenith Media NP4 0DQ

Contents

About the writers

Erica Roberts is a former paediatric oncologist. As an Anglican priest, she has been passionate about her role as city chaplain for older people in Southampton. Supporting this work, she founded the charity Caraway in 2019 which has worked in close partnership with Anna Chaplaincy ever since. This summer she and her husband 'retired' to Devon.

April McIntyre lives in Derbyshire with her husband Mike and serves as an Anglican lay minister. In recent years, she has been using writing as part of her Christian ministry. Now published locally and nationally, she is a member of the Association of Christian Writers and self-published a small book of reflections and poems in 2022.

'Tricia Williams is a freelance writer and editor with a passion for helping people engage with God's word. She has a special interest in the spiritual support of people living with dementia and is the author of *God's Not Forgotten Me* (Cascade Books, 2022). She is married to Emlyn (also a writer for *Bible Reflections for Older People*)and has two adult children and one granddaughter.

Angela Tilby worked for the BBC as a producer of religious programmes for 22 years. Ordained in 1997, she became a tutor at Westcott House in Cambridge. After some years as a parish priest she moved to Oxford as diocesan canon of Christ Church Cathedral. She writes for the *Church Times*, broadcasts frequently on Radio 4's *Thought for the Day* and is now a canon emeritus of Christ Church Cathedral.

From the Editor

Welcome!

This issue spans the season of Remembrance. When Remembrance Sunday and Armistice Day come, I'm sure our screens will be full of images from the commemorations of the 80th anniversary of VE Day on 8 May. Inevitably there are fewer and fewer veterans on parade each year, but the proud nonagenarians in Whitehall, and at war memorials around the country, are a poignant and humbling reminder of the courageous sacrifices made in the name of service, peace and freedom.

Last November I visited the National Memorial Arboretum in Staffordshire. A stunningly beautiful site hosting over 400 memorials and 25,000 trees, it's described as a '150 acre living landscape'. Planting only began in 1996, on the site of an old quarry. Officially opened in 2001, the Arboretum now, rightly, attracts over 300,000 visitors a year.

From the Armed Forces Memorial to the brightly painted carousel horse of the Showmen's Guild, the hundreds of memorials pay tribute to members not only of the armed forces, but of the emergency services and civilian organisations. At the heart of the arboretum is the Millennium Chapel of Peace and Forgiveness, the only place in the country where the Act of Remembrance is observed daily.

The National Memorial Arboretum is a remarkable embodiment of peace, reconciliation and remembrance, and on a site once scarred by decades of quarrying, the healing of the very earth beneath our feet.

Go well

Eley

Using these reflections

Perhaps you have always had a special time each day for reading the Bible and praying. But now, as you grow older, you are finding it more difficult to keep to a regular pattern or find it harder to concentrate. Or, maybe you've never done this before. Whatever your situation, these Bible reflections aim to help you take a few moments to read God's Word and pray whenever you have time or feel that would be helpful.

When to read them

You might use these Bible reflections in the morning or last thing at night, but they work at any time of day. There are 40 reflections here, grouped around four themes, by four different writers. Each one includes some verses from the Bible, a reflection to help you in your own thinking about God, and a prayer suggestion. The reflections aren't dated, so it doesn't matter if you don't want to read every day. The Bible verses are printed, but you might prefer to follow them in your own Bible.

How to read them

- **Take time** to quieten yourself, becoming aware of God's presence, asking him to speak to you through the Bible and the reflection.
- **Read** the Bible verses and the reflection:
  - What do you especially like or find helpful in these verses?
  - What might God be saying to you through this reading?
  - Is there something to pray about or thank God for?
- **Pray**. Each reflection includes a prayer suggestion. You might like to pray for yourself or take the opportunity to think about and pray for others.

Tramping with Jesus

Erica Roberts

‘As they talked and discussed these things, Jesus himself suddenly came and began walking with them’ (Luke 24:15, NIV).

In many stories about Jesus, we find him walking: around Lake Galilee, through Samaria en route to Judea, north towards Caesarea Philippi, across the river Jordan and always, of course, walking purposefully towards his final journey into Jerusalem. In Luke 24, although initially unrecognised, we join Jesus as he walks towards Emmaus with two of his followers.

On a recent trip to visit family in New Zealand, I was fortunate to go on a three-day hike, or tramp as they are known by the locals, carrying all our provisions and staying in walking huts along the way. With a chronic knee problem, this tramp felt like a significant achievement, and sharpened into focus the surrounding beauty, the people we met and the physical demands of a long walk.

The following notes are a result of my reflections over those three days as I imagined Jesus tramping with me, enjoying the scenery, joining in conversations and, as he did with his disciples, teaching me more about living as one of his followers. I invite you to join me on this tramp with Jesus over the coming days.

Matthew 4:19–20 (NIV)

Anticipation

'Come, follow me,' Jesus said, 'and I will send you out to fish for people.' At once they left their nets and followed him.

I wonder what gives you that buzz of anticipation. Can you remember daydreaming about a long-planned holiday, poring over travel guides as the excitement builds or wondering what to pack? Of course, that wonderful feeling of anticipation often comes from the smaller things in life, waiting for a good friend to visit or a package to arrive, or perhaps imagining a square of chocolate melting in your mouth.

Called to follow Jesus, the disciples had no time to plan or pack a bag. We are told that they left their nets at once and followed him. However, they were not unprepared; they had been watching Jesus, talking about him and listening to him. I suspect God was already creating a longing in their hearts that was crying out to be met. In stepping out to follow Jesus, each day of their journey ahead would have been filled with glorious anticipation, as Jesus gradually revealed more about himself to them.

As we spend time with Jesus, I wonder how you feel about the journey ahead. I hope you're also filled with glorious anticipation, unbridled curiosity and a willingness to go where Jesus leads. It is a great adventure.

■ **PRAYER**

Lord Jesus, knowing our fears and our doubts, we pray for hearts full of glorious anticipation for the journey ahead with you. Amen

Luke 9:3 (NIV)

The baggage we carry

[Jesus] told them: 'Take nothing for the journey – no staff, no bag, no bread, no money, no extra shirt.'

Before we set off on our three-day tramp in New Zealand, I thought very carefully about what to pack. I didn't want to carry any more than I needed, knowing how tired my legs would become as the miles stretched out, and yet I needed to ensure I had enough for the journey, including food, a first-aid kit and a head-torch.

When Jesus sent his disciples out, he instructed them to take nothing. I honestly can't imagine taking absolutely nothing with me; in fact, it doesn't even seem very responsible. However, Jesus wanted his disciples to depend on the hospitality of strangers and, in their vulnerability, enable others to bless them with generosity. In return, the disciples shared the most precious gift they had with them, the good news of Jesus.

Sometimes we are encumbered with a metaphorical bag that weighs us down. In Hebrews we are reminded to 'throw off everything that hinders' (12:1). We are burdened by our anxieties, weighed down by our guilt and entangled with shame. The author in Hebrews continues by encouraging us to 'fix our eyes on Jesus, the pioneer and perfecter of faith' (v. 2). Tramping with Jesus means we can lay down our burdens, lift our heads high and confidently step out with faith along the path ahead.

■ **PRAYER**

Loving Jesus, help us keep our eyes firmly fixed on you. Amen

Psalm 77:19 (NIV)

Making footprints

Your path led through the sea, your way through the mighty waters, though your footprints were not seen.

I love the sensation of sand under my feet as I walk along an untouched beach. Looking back, a single line of footprints is visible, which lasts only a moment when the sand is wet and certainly no longer than it takes for the tide to rise and wash them away. Tramping in New Zealand came with strict instructions to leave nothing behind, including bagging up our rubbish to take away. Therefore, leaving our footprints, albeit for a moment, left only the briefest memory that we had passed that way as our footprints intermingled with others – young, old and all shapes and sizes.

Our psalm today refers to God's invisible footprints, despite the visible consequences of God's actions creating a life-changing path through the waters, referring to the parting of the Red Sea, as Moses led the Israelites to freedom. In our journey of faith, we may not see God's footprints, but the impact of his presence is so often known as lives are transformed and guidance revealed.

Like Moses, we need to trust that God will not only be our guide but also intervene to clear the path ahead of seemingly insurmountable obstacles. I wonder where you hope to see the impact of God's footprints today. Ask him now for what you need.

■ **PRAYER**

Gracious Father, thank you for the footprints you leave in our lives. Amen

Exodus 13:17a (NIV)

Detours

When Pharaoh let the people go, God did not lead them on the road through the Philistine country, though that was shorter.

Some of our New Zealand tramp was dependent on the tide-times. Not starting early enough one morning, I was disgruntled to miss the long and beautiful walk across a beach at sunrise and to then discover that the detour both was longer and included a steep hill. Nevertheless, the detour brought unexpected joys, a wonderful footbridge and glorious early-morning birdsong.

Detours are unexpected and usually unwelcome. Think about Dorothy in *The Wizard of Oz.* She hoped to find a land over the rainbow, where troubles would melt like lemon drops. In fact, her challenging adventures through Oz shaped and matured her and gave her a better appreciation of her home in Kansas.

The same is true for our lives, when something unexpected explodes into our daily routine, causing upheaval and unwelcome changes. These times can be hard, even painful to navigate, but in the same way that God protected the Israelites as they took a long detour through the wilderness, so God promises to protect and guide us through the detours in our own lives.

Detours may be confusing, complicated and challenging, but through them our lives can be shaped, as we learn to depend on God, and place our trust in him for the way ahead.

■ **PRAYER**

God, our guide and protector, help us to trust you in the detours of our lives. Amen

Psalm 119:133 (NIV)

Carrying poles

Direct my footsteps according to your word; let no sin rule over me.

Living for many years with a damaged knee, I have discovered how useful walking poles can be, particularly on those treacherous descents. Not only do they take weight off your knees, but they stabilise your core muscles and are useful to test the terrain ahead. Making use of poles engages many of our muscles, providing a good whole-body workout.

In our journeys through life, it can be easy to 'go it alone', not turning to God for help and guidance. We have a faith, we pray, but we leave God out of our daily lives. In our psalm today we are reminded that our footsteps can be directed by God's word. Carrying God's word with us throughout life, being steeped in the stories of God, memorising verses to encourage and comfort us when times are tough, is like carrying walking poles.

Scripture guides us on those treacherous descents when we feel anxious and afraid; God's word helps us test the terrain ahead when we are making significant decisions; and the truth we find in scripture gives us the confidence to hold our heads high as we move through the complexities of life. Moreover, being grounded in God's word maintains our spiritual fitness, so that when we stumble, we are equipped to deal with unexpected obstacles in our path.

■ **PRAYER**

Read a favourite verse and give thanks to God for the gift of his word.

Psalm 25:4–5 (NIV)

Signposts

Show me your ways, Lord, teach me your paths. Guide me in your truth and teach me, for you are God my Saviour, and my hope is in you all day long.

Navigation has changed dramatically over the years. I suspect you'll remember poring over a map when planning a long journey. And what about the local A–Z, always to be found dog-eared in the car ready for navigation to a particular address? In our youth, many of us will also have learnt to use a compass alongside a map. Nowadays of course, we just follow a satnav or a map on our phones: extremely efficient, but we can easily lose the wider geographical perspective.

On our tramp in New Zealand, we were fortunate to follow clear and efficient signposts, found in all the National Parks, with alternative routes offered depending on tide-times and weather. Good directions bring confidence and enable the journey to go smoothly.

Along our lifepath there will be twists, turns and signposts. Like the psalmist, we trust that God will show us the path to take. I believe that God loves to be creative in the way he directs us, speaking through the beauty of his creation, revealing himself in scripture, prayer or wise counsel from another. However, we will only hear the whisper of his voice if we choose to be attentive and make space to listen.

■ **PRAYER**

Creator God, help us to be attentive to your voice today. Amen

1 Kings 2:1, 7 (NIV)

Companions on the way

When the time drew near for David to die, he gave a charge to Solomon his son... 'But show kindness to the sons of Barzillai of Gilead and let them be among those who eat at your table. They stood by me when I fled from your brother Absalom.'

I love hearing stories from those who walk the Camino de Santiago, pilgrims journeying towards their goal of Santiago de Compostela, often travelling alone but meeting companions on the way – sharing stories, mutual support and encouragement. During our Antipodean tramp, enjoying a moment with a fellow walker was one of the joys, discovering something of their lives, sharing advice and even watching a sunset together.

Today we hear about Barzillai, perhaps my favourite hidden biblical character, an older man who offered support and companionship to David on his flight from Absalom. Do read the story in 2 Samuel 17:27–29 and 19:31–39. David is so grateful for Barzillai's help that on his return he invites him to Jerusalem, where Barzillai can be provided for in his older years. With wisdom, Barzillai declines, acknowledging that he will be more comfortable near his own family, but suggests a younger man, Kimham, should go instead, providing an opportunity of a lifetime.

Spend some time giving thanks for companions that God has placed alongside you, those who have brought solace or support, for a moment, or maybe a lifetime.

■ **PRAYER**

Lord Jesus, show us who we could offer companionship to today. Amen

Matthew 26:26 (NIV)

Capturing memories

While they were eating, Jesus took bread, and when he had given thanks, he broke it and gave it to his disciples, saying, 'Take and eat; this is my body.'

Throughout Jesus' adult ministry he captivated his audiences with stories that were grounded in everyday life, stories that stretched their imagination and challenged their understanding of God. Stories such as the kingdom of heaven being like a mustard seed, a lost son who is welcomed home despite squandering his inheritance or that wonderful image of the bread and wine immortalised in the story of the last supper.

Stories like these are memorable and are captured in our imagination. We have our own stories of God's faithfulness that can be passed on to others, just as the stories of Jesus have been passed down through the centuries. One story I share came as an auditory reminder of God's compassionate care as I heard a bird singing outside, a moment that wonderfully spoke to me of God's goodness at a time when I felt particularly vulnerable after a period of ill health and dependence on others.

Just as we love to capture memories of our lives in a photo, or perhaps a journal, so we can also capture our faith memories to share with others. I wonder if you could share some of your memories of God's faithfulness with someone else today.

■ **PRAYER**

Living Lord Jesus, as a master storyteller, help us to share our own stories of your hope and love. Amen

Psalm 121:1–2 (NIV)

Pausing

I lift up my eyes to the mountains – where does my help come from? My help comes from the Lord, the Maker of heaven and earth.

I wonder how often we are fully present in the moment, not distracted by the world around us or preoccupied by events unfolding in our own lives. I love watching my new grandson gaze intently at his mother, a smile breaking out across his face. Nothing will distract that gaze which is building trust and deepening the bond of love.

In Psalm 121 we can imagine the author pausing, embracing the beauty of the mountains. It is in the pausing that the psalmist has space to consider this life-changing question, 'Where does my help come from?' It is in the pausing that God reveals himself in profound ways, and we are fortunate that the psalmist recorded his revelation for us.

I slowly recited Psalm 121 as I paused at the foot of Aoraki, Mount Cook, hidden in the mist, and yet still imposing in its grandeur. As I paused and waited awhile, God reminded me that he, like Aoraki, may not be clearly visible, but he is and always will be present. I wonder if you could find a moment today to pause, lay aside any distractions and read Psalm 121 slowly, asking God your own question and see what he says in return.

■ PRAYER

'The Lord will watch over your coming and going both now and forevermore' (Psalm 121:8). Amen

Matthew 2:1 (NIV)

Arriving

After Jesus was born in Bethlehem in Judea, during the time of King Herod, Magi from the east came to Jerusalem.

After a long journey, it is wonderful to arrive. Following our three-day tramp in New Zealand, we were extremely dusty with weary legs. A hot shower, a freshly prepared meal and clean sheets rather than our sleeping bags were readily welcomed. The tramp had taken us to places of outstanding beauty, we had met some interesting people, exchanged fascinating stories, and yet it was still good to arrive.

The journey of the Magi must have been exhausting and dangerous. Although they travelled for weeks searching for Jesus, we know little of their journey, the beauty or wildness of the terrain, the strangers they met or companionship they shared. For the Magi the focus was the destination, and they were determined to go to great lengths to find this new king.

Their destination is also our destination. Jesus was waiting for them, as he is waiting for us. How wonderful that Jesus tramps with us day by day, sustaining, encouraging and guiding us, and yet Jesus is also waiting to welcome us home when we arrive at our heavenly destination. One day, like the Magi, we will come face to face with Jesus and our response, like theirs, will be to bow down and worship.

■ PRAYER

Heavenly Father, help us to have hearts full of hope and anticipation for the day when we will see you face to face. Amen

Jars of clay

April McIntyre

I grew up in Stoke-on-Trent, on the edge of the Potteries, so perhaps it's not surprising that early in adult life, God seemed to be showing me a 'jar of clay': small, chipped, neither decorative nor very useful. This pot was me. I wondered how God could possibly be interested in such an embarrassing object but found my answer in 2 Corinthians 4, where Paul explains how God uses such unpromising containers to accommodate his glorious treasures. This picture has inspired me throughout my life.

Now, as I grow older, I am all too aware of the fragility and failings of our human bodies and minds, yet I also realise that the Master Potter is both ingenious, compassionate and able to work out his purposes through our very weaknesses and frailty: 'Not by might nor by power, but by my Spirit,' says the Lord Almighty (Zechariah 4:6).

The reflections that follow explore the tensions between our flawed and vulnerable humanity and the glorious treasures God has placed within us, treasures both to delight us and to share. I hope they will inspire and encourage you on your own journeys.

2 Corinthians 4:7 (NIV)

In jars of clay

But we have this treasure in jars of clay to show that this all-surpassing power is from God and not from us.

I wonder if Paul sometimes looked at his body, scarred from beatings, hard-living and constant travel, and wondered what had happened to Saul of Tarsus, his brilliant younger self. Did he see only a 'jar of clay', nearing the end of its usefulness?

In Paul's day, clay pots of all shapes and sizes were used for cooking, lighting and storage. Among these commonplace containers, a few might also be used to hide precious objects or coins from thieves or enemy attack.

Paul uses the clay jar as a metaphor for the spiritual life. Clay represents humanity, ordinariness, vulnerability and mortality into which the spirit of life is breathed. But unlike so many mass-produced pots from modern factories, made on an assembly line so that each piece is identical, the jars of clay pictured by Paul would have been handmade. Big or small, decorative or functional, cracked or flawed, each was unique and would have its own part to play.

Imagine that you are a jar of clay. How do you see yourself? What are your uses? Why not find or draw a picture of your pot and let God speak to you through it?

■ PRAYER

Loving God, help us to see ourselves as you see us and realise how valuable we are to you. Amen

2 Corinthians 4:6 (NIV)

Treasures of light

For God, who said, 'Let light shine out of darkness,' made his light shine in our hearts to give us the light of the knowledge of God's glory displayed in the face of Christ.

Can you imagine Paul watching a flame dancing on a dingy, clay oil lamp as he tries to convey to the Corinthians his passionate conviction that God's creative light can shine out from ordinary, imperfect Christians? This is the treasure he mentions in verse 7 (which we looked at yesterday).

Our 'jars of clay' can be filled not only with gospel glory but also with a treasure hoard of grace, gifts and blessings. In addition, God's very presence abides within us, like a living flame, purifying and transforming us.

This illumination affects not just our understanding but the way we live and love, our motivations and relationships, our hopes and dreams. Jesus himself said we must let this light shine out so that others may see our good deeds and praise God (Matthew 5:14–16).

How do you feel about the light of the gospel hidden inside you? Does it give you deep, inner joy and excitement or feel like a heavy responsibility? Talk to God about your reactions.

■ PRAYER

Almighty God, you call us to be lights to our world. Help us find ways to reflect your light each day. Amen

2 Corinthians 4:7–9 (NIV, abridged)

Not abandoned

We have this treasure in jars of clay... We are hard pressed on every side, but not crushed; perplexed, but not in despair; persecuted, but not abandoned; struck down, but not destroyed.

In my early 20s, I began to suffer badly with frequent migraine attacks: crushing headaches, sensitivity to light and noise, being sick, becoming depressed. This was to dominate my life for the next three decades or so and, though new medications helped, the effect on career and relationships was significant.

Yet I was a Christian. I knew there were many good things in me, but I felt trapped in my defective clay jar. Sometimes I couldn't help hating the way I was. Was it my fault? Was it God's? How could I follow Jesus when I felt like this?

Paul, however, urges us to keep trusting our creator, even when we are hard-pressed, perplexed or struck down, even in our pain, with our heads down the loo!

For God's love never fails. He is a friend who is always with us so that we never have to face our struggles alone. Why not talk to God about anything impacting your life today?

■ PRAYER

Father God, when I am hurting and just want to give up, be with me and hold me close. In the darkness and despair, help me to trust that I am still your beloved child. Amen

Isaiah 64:8 (NIV)

Master Potter

Yet you, Lord, are our Father. We are the clay, you are the potter; we are all the work of your hand.

Have you ever watched *The Great Pottery Throw Down* on the television? Filmed at Gladstone Pottery, only a few miles from where I grew up in Stoke-on-Trent, it is an annual knock-out competition to find the best amateur potter. Contestants must tackle demanding challenges such as designing, throwing, slab building, glazing and firing. Creating their own unique pieces, contestants often emerge weary, smeared with clay but bubbling with delight.

Being creative is often a messy business and potting can be unpredictable, even heart-breaking, especially when precious pots explode in the kiln. Scripture reminds us that God is the Master Potter and we are the clay in his hands. God is utterly committed to his work and not afraid to get his hands dirty, holding a plan in mind yet allowing his creation to evolve and grow.

Are we willing to surrender ourselves into the Potter's hands and cooperate in achieving his vision? Can we trust him with the sharp tools that form and shape us?

Isaiah assures us that the Master Potter is also our Father so even the cutting and firing are aspects of his love for us.

■ **PRAYER**

Thank you, Master Potter, for the time and patience you spend on our formation. Thank you that we can trust the hands that hold us. Amen

Genesis 2:7 (NIV)

Made from dust

Then the Lord God formed a man from the dust of the ground and breathed into his nostrils the breath of life, and the man became a living being.

I cradled the cool clay in my hands, alone, on retreat. I began to knead and squeeze. Slowly, an elongated shape emerged: a swollen face, limbs stretched stiff by its sides. It was Jesus, awaiting the tomb.

I lavished my love upon this small, clay body, doing what the women longed to do on Easter morning, anointing Jesus' body with perfume, tears and love. Yet, as I worked, I found myself also thinking of my father who had died some time ago, suddenly, after dinner at our house. Now, with time to reflect and remember, I could express through my fingers a lifetime's gratitude and grief and say goodbye.

Ecclesiastes 3:20 says that we all come from dust and to dust we return. Dust, earth, clay. Yet this is not the end. For in Jesus, God, too, became a human being, a jar of clay. So God knows first-hand what it is to feel and suffer, to pass through life, death and on into eternity.

If we are willing, this same God can fill our own jars of clay to overflowing with resurrection power that will take us beyond dust and ashes and into life everlasting.

■ **PRAYER**

Breathe on me, breath of God, that I might live today and for eternity. Amen

Jeremiah 18:3–6 (NIV, abridged)

The potter's house

So I went down to the potter's house, and I saw him working at the wheel. But the pot he was shaping from the clay was marred in his hands; so the potter formed it into another pot, shaping it as seemed best to him. Then the word of the Lord came to me. He said, '… Like clay in the hand of the potter, so are you in my hand.'

Around 600 BC, the young prophet Jeremiah walked down through the Potsherd Gate, south of Jerusalem, to the area where potters worked, where broken pots were dumped and kilns kept safely outside the city. These were troubled times in the kingdom of Judah as people turned away from God and the threat from mighty Assyria increased. Surely God's judgement must soon fall.

What God shows Jeremiah, however, is a potter working on a wheel, drawing up the clay with sensitive hands, feeling his way forwards. Then there's a wobble: the walls of the pot shiver and the whole thing collapses. But, undeterred, the potter scrapes up the clay, kneads it back into a ball, slaps it back on to the wheel and starts again.

There is no anger or frustration from the potter. Mistakes and problems are all part of the creative process, even for an expert. Even for God? There is always another chance if we remain obedient and open in God's hands.

■ **PRAYER**

Thank you, loving God, that though things often go wrong in our lives, there is always another chance. Amen

John 1:14a (NIV)

Incarnation

The Word became flesh and made his dwelling among us. We have seen his glory.

There is a moving description in Isaiah 53 that paints a picture of God's chosen one. This helps us understand something of the meaning of the incarnation, when the glory of God was poured into a mortal vessel with 'no beauty or majesty to attract us… nothing in his appearance that we should desire him' (Isaiah 53:2).

Throughout their history, the Jews believed that God inhabited special places of meeting such as the Tabernacle or the great temples. In Jesus, we see God inhabiting, being incarnate in, basic, human clay. There was nothing to mark Jesus out as special, yet he carried our sorrows and burdens all the way to the cross so that we could be forgiven, healed and brought close to God. This truly is 'good news'.

Because Jesus was 'made flesh', he knows what it feels like to be human. This means that we can identify with him as a fellow jar of clay and trust him, not just as our Saviour but as our friend. We can enter into his sufferings as he enters into ours and, as we look to the future, we can be sure that Jesus has prepared a place for us to abide with him forever.

■ **PRAYER**

Jesus, suffering Saviour, we offer you our gratitude and love. Amen

2 Corinthians 4:16–17 (NIV)

Renewed

Therefore we do not lose heart. Though outwardly we are wasting away, yet inwardly we are being renewed day by day. For our light and momentary troubles are achieving for us an eternal glory that far outweighs them all.

I was in my 20s when I first started thinking about jars of clay. I pictured a small, dumpy, ugly pot, stained and chipped. It had already been fired so it couldn't be started afresh. Yet, as I looked, I realised that something was happening on the inside. The sides were being smoothed and decorated as if the potter was making a new pot from the inside out.

Work progressed. The pot became lighter and thinner so that I was worried it might break, but at the same time the inner walls were being reinforced with a gleaming mesh of fine fibres and, even through the cracks, a light shone outwards. One day, the outer pot would break and be discarded. Only then would the true beauty of the inner pot be revealed.

So don't lose heart, says Paul. Even as we get older, plagued by aching limbs or failing eyesight, God is renewing us from the inside out. And awaiting us will be 'an eternal glory' that will eclipse every trouble and heartache.

■ **PRAYER**

'Create in me a pure heart, O God, and renew a steadfast spirit within me' (Psalm 51:10).

2 Corinthians 12:9–10 (NIV, abridged)

Through the cracks

'My grace is sufficient for you, for my power is made perfect in weakness'... For when I am weak, then I am strong.

I sometimes wonder whether I would have liked Paul! He can seem so sure of himself, so driven. Towards the end of 2 Corinthians, however, he confesses that his self-confidence and 'conceit' needed to be kept in check by 'a thorn in the flesh', perhaps chronic illness or ongoing persecution. What an important lesson this is.

God's secret weapon is the hiding of his grace and blessings in the clay pots of ordinary believers, those who are willing to let go of ambition and achievement and rely on God's resurrection power within. Ironically, the weaker the vessel, the more the light of the glorious gospel is able to shine through. The more battered and cracked the pot, the more God's grace radiates outwards.

This means that we don't have to strive to be heroes or doers of great deeds, for God is more than happy for us to let go and just 'be' with him as friends. Our hang-ups and sufferings can encourage us to depend on God rather than ourselves, and as others see the light shining through our cracks, perhaps they too will be touched by God's saving grace.

■ PRAYER

Loving God, here I am in my weakness. Be close to me today and fill me with your grace and resurrection power. Amen

Colossians 1:27 (NIV)

Glory

To them God has chosen to make known among the Gentiles the glorious riches of this mystery, which is Christ in you, the hope of glory.

I look around my study and notice several ceramic objects: a dog with a badly glued ear, a woodpecker with a broken tail and an old red/orange enamelled sweet jar that belonged to my nana. I treasure them not for their looks or value but because they are part of my family history and part of me.

I believe that God looks on us in a similar way, with warmth and perhaps a wry smile. For we are precious to him not just as potential evangelists, helpers or worshippers but because we are family, his own beloved children.

Throughout our lives, there will be many struggles that limit what we can be and do, but God gives each one of us special treasures to share. They don't have to be spectacular. Discovering an insight from scripture, baking a tasty cake for a friend, spending time really listening as someone tells their story, responding to family or carers with a smile or word of thanks. Sometimes, all we can do is sit back, close our eyes and know that God still abides deep within us. But this is enough.

■ **PRAYER**

Creator God, thank you for your loving presence within me. Show me, each day, how I may share your glorious treasures. In Jesus' name. Amen

The Gift of Years

Debbie Thrower is the founder of BRF Ministries' Anna Chaplaincy for Older People. She retired in late 2023 and is now a vice president of BRF Ministries.

Visit **annachaplaincy.org.uk** to find out more.

Debbie writes…

Welcome!

You know those quick-fire questionnaires in magazines, inviting you to choose between, say: mountain or beach, custard or cream, Leonard Cohen or Bob Dylan? For me it would be beach, cream, Cohen.

One of my favourite Leonard Cohen songs, 'Anthem', features the memorable line about cracks being the very place where light gets in. I wonder if it's an allusion to Paul's second letter to the Corinthians and his promise: 'But we have this treasure in jars of clay, to show that the surpassing power belongs to God and not to us' (2 Corinthians 4:7, ESV).

April McIntyre focuses on that wonderful message of hope from 2 Corinthians in her series 'Jars of clay'. We have hope not in spite of but *because of* our human imperfections.

I recently watched an old DVD of Leonard Cohen at a London concert recorded in his later years. He was still full of charisma; his trademark sonorous voice in fine form despite advancing years. 'Anthem' continued to strike a deep chord with the audience. When Cohen died in 2016 we lost a man whose wisdom was hard-earned and an artist who'd shared his spiritual journey throughout his long writing career, enriching many millions of his fans along the way.

I hope you, too, find much to make you hopeful in these pages.

With my best wishes.

Debbie

Music and memory

Frances Attwood is an Anna Chaplain with a passion for using music in her ministry. She has a background in teaching music, and then she became a music therapist. Her interest in dementia came about when she was running a number of community music groups. She eventually moved into chaplaincy, 'Partly,' she explains, 'because in the music therapy profession, you're not allowed to share your faith, and I felt that was the most important thing I had to offer.'

Frances is a regular visitor to a local care home in Southbourne near Bournemouth. 'I always thought I would like to take my violin in with me,' she says, 'and I've found it really useful.' Right from the beginning, she wanted to work with people who can't get out of their rooms, and that's what she does.

'I'm currently visiting a 100-year-old who is probably in the last stages of life but I always say, "Would you like me to play you something?" and the reply comes, "Oh, yes, please!" And if that's all I do, I think it's really special. Then on the other end, I've been visiting somebody who probably doesn't have a personal faith, but music opens up conversation; it opens up the opportunity to talk about things in a very immediate way.'

Frances also runs a reminiscence group at a nearby United Reformed Church, where music has always been an important element. 'We have a theme,' she explains. 'It might be work, or travel, or school, for example, and the songs definitely stir up memories for people. It's a lovely way of engaging them in the topic, but also just the sheer enjoyment of singing is lovely.

'One of the things I've always found about using music is that it works at whatever level. So if somebody's nonverbal, that doesn't matter at all. They can be tapping their foot or nodding their head, or sometimes I will give them percussion instruments and they can play along. I see some people who have been completely silent for months or even years, mouthing all the words of a song.

'In the reminiscence sessions, some of the family carers stay, and I feel that it's really helpful for them to see these lovely glimpses of what they've known the person to be in the past. And for people with dementia, who are losing many abilities, it's a really empowering thing to offer them, something they can still do. So it's a wonderful enabling tool. I just love using it.'

Researchers are developing their understanding of why music therapy is so powerful. They have done all sorts of scientific experiments, where they put sensors on different parts of the head to measure brain activity in response to different stimuli. Whereas they used to think music just affected the right side of the brain, the creative side, they now realise that it activates all sorts of areas of the brain.

Frances explains: 'Different aspects of music – rhythm, harmony, melody, movement in relation to the music – affect different parts of the brain and that's why it is so powerful. Because it affects different parts of the brain, it also then stimulates other brain functions that may be fading. So, for example, speech: somebody who can't speak can sing all the words of a song that they knew from their youth. It's just amazing. Similarly, I heard a neurologist speak about Parkinson's disease. He said when somebody finds it really difficult to signal to their legs to move in order to walk, if they're listening to music on headphones, they can walk completely fluently. So music is activating, triggering, stimulating the whole brain.'

Some years ago Frances went to a conference about the creative arts and dementia. She still vividly remembers one particular story shared at the event. 'A woman who ran a singing group said there was a woman in the group who hadn't spoken for 18 months. Then one day the group leader happened to hit on a particular song that was very special to the woman, who, to everyone's amazement and delight, proceeded to stand up and perform it to the group. The following week, her husband came and told the group leader that after they got home, his wife said, "I'd like to bake a cake." So with his help, she did! Again, it was that stimulation from the song that reactivated other parts of the brain. So, yes, it's really powerful.'

Frances has written a new Easy Guide about setting up a singing group for older people, available for free on the Anna Chaplainy website. Go to **annachaplaincy.org.uk/easy-guides**.

Adoration

To sit in silence could be enough.
Prolonged stillness would show
due reverence to a symbolic sacrament.
But here, as the tabernacle door is opened,
and holiness exposed,
Love beckons,
and in this true presence
we fall to our knees.

Such beauty demands humility,
invokes submission to this mystery.
Tears fall freely in adoration,
hearts fall unfathomably in love
with the One who offers the reality
of an eternal embrace.

Maggie Jackson (used with kind permission)

Maggie Jackson is a spiritual director, retreat guide and poet. Maggie trained in Ignatian spirituality and was a retreat guide at the Community of the Resurrection in Mirfield from 2010 to 2019. She has published poems in several anthologies, journals and on websites, has given public poetry readings and led workshops linking poetry and spirituality. Maggie was Poet in Residence at Mirfield in 2017 and this poem comes from the collection *Offertory*, which is the published outcome of her residency.

'Some poems emerged from prayer,' she says, 'others from observation or conversation, and prolonged silence stirred memories which demanded to be shared poetically.'

(*Offertory* is available from Mirfield Publications: **mirfield.org.uk**)

Embracing humanity

Last December Julia Burton-Jones, training and development lead for Anna Chaplaincy, wrote a personal reflection on Advent for the BRF Ministries website. She wrote about some of the things that had struck her while reading *Embracing Humanity*, the 2024 Advent book from BRF Ministries by Isabelle Hamley, with a small group at her church. She said that it was 'full of riches' and that she was 'glad we chose to read it'. Here Julia shares some of those riches in the hope that they will resonate with you too.

Space to breathe

In the midst of the busyness and stress of the run-up to Christmas, it was a great joy to be treated by Anna Chaplains in Rochester Diocese to a 'Space to breathe' day to mark ten years of Anna Chaplaincy in Kent. Cudham and Downe Anna Chaplains John and Kim Curle prepared a day for Anna Chaplains and Anna Friends to spend together, being generously looked after while enjoying Christmas crafts and a time of worship. It was a wonderful oasis of peace and creativity, and unusual for the team to be on the receiving end of such loving kindness when we tend to be the ones offering such events to others.

'Space to breathe' got me thinking about day three in *Embracing Humanity* entitled 'Related and dependent'. Isabelle talks about our need for one another, going right back to the story of Eve being created from Adam in Genesis.

We so easily hide the bit of being human which is about needing others behind a wall of self-sufficiency and autonomy, and in this I know I am guilty; I love giving Christmas gifts but am less good at receiving them from others.

I was heartened to read in *Embracing Humanity* 'to be dependent is not to be weak, less adult, or less human. Being dependent, needing others, is profoundly, deeply and beautifully human'. Jesus did not 'take flesh' as a fully grown adult but as a dependent infant. For older people who have reached a stage of frailty, depending on others for their care, this is a positive message.

Fragile and vulnerable

Day four in *Embracing Humanity* is equally relevant to people living with dementia and disability in their later years, as it looks at Jesus being 'fragile and vulnerable'. Jesus became fragile by taking our human form, but Isabelle also explores the vulnerability in the heart of God which stems from love and compassion for the human race. We share this vulnerability as we are also called to be compassionate. 'True compassion goes hand in hand with vulnerability, because I can only be compassionate when I open my heart to love another and feel their pain, their brokenness, their struggle.'

Embracing our embodied selves

Day two of *Embracing Humanity* is entitled 'Embodied'. The subtitle of the book is 'a journey towards becoming flesh' so the focus is on what it means that Jesus lived with us in a human body. The dualism in western culture between the body and the soul, where the soul is seen as more important, is challenged by Isabelle through reference to scriptures showing the importance of the whole person. Jesus the bread of life gave us his body – 'unless you eat the flesh of the son of man and drink his blood, you have no life in you' (John 6:53).

Bodies are precious to God, and not despised. My many years of working alongside older people and those affected by dementia has underlined for me the preciousness of our bodies at every stage in life.

When words fail in later dementia, we can still use our bodies and spirits to worship God and participate in the rituals of our faith. Our bodies retain the memory of moving in response to God's love when joining with the church family in singing, praying and taking Communion. This is a wonderful demonstration of the Spirit of God at work in the whole person when cognition is diminishing, and it speaks to me of how the word becoming flesh was part of God's plan for our broken world.

Julia Burton-Jones joined BRF Ministries in May 2020. Since 2015 she has pioneered Anna Chaplaincy in Kent and South-East London. With a background in adult learning in ageing and dementia, her role as training and development lead includes writing and delivering courses for those exploring being an Anna Chaplain or Anna Friend, and ongoing ministerial education for the growing Anna Chaplaincy network.

For more information about *Embracing Humanity* go to **brfonline.org.uk/embracing-humanity**

Time to serve

'Tricia Williams

It's strange realising that now I am one of *those* older people! Gradually, you notice younger people placing you in that category. 'More patience needed, doesn't understand technology, smile and be nice.' It can be easy – or the path of least resistance – to simply accept this. But while we may have less energy and be slower in our thinking, God doesn't expect us just to sit back and let others serve us. He has work for us to do.

Surprisingly, being older might bring a greater liberty to serve. Jenny Joseph's poem, 'When I am… old… I shall wear purple'* mischievously highlights the increased freedom you may feel in these later years. As Christians, that might be in talking to others about God and our faith.

This series explores some of the ways in which we can serve God – and others – at this time of our lives: through listening; in telling the younger generation about our faith; through prayer; through our trust in God; in being hopeful for the future. As you read, listen for God's prompting and the Spirit's leading as you seek to serve him today.

> *'The Son of Man did not come to be served, but to serve.'*
> MARK 10:45 (NIV)

* *Warning*, Jenny Joseph (1961)

Ecclesiastes 3:1–8 (NIV, abridged)

A time for everything

There is a time for everything… a time to be born and a time to die… a time to weep and a time to laugh… to mourn… to dance… to embrace… to refrain from embracing… a time to tear… a time to mend… to be silent… to speak… a time for war and a time for peace.

Take a few moments to reflect back over your life – times of celebration and mourning, good times and sad times. Now, at this time, as we face the challenges and opportunities of later life, how might God want us to serve him?

One Sunday, at the end of a church service, I remember Mary who told me at some length about difficulties in her life. As we were parting, she said, 'Thank you for talking with me… you've really helped me.' But I had hardly said a word. There are times to be silent and just be there. Think about the people who come to your door or those you chat with at church. As we listen to others – their griefs and anxieties, their joys and sorrows – our listening and presence can bring comfort and encouragement. Whatever our age, we can still be present with others as they journey through the ups and downs of life described in these verses.

■ PRAYER

What is it time for in your life today? Ask God to help you serve him as you walk with others, seeking to bring his comfort and encouragement.

Psalm 71:17–18 (NIV)

When I am old and grey...

Since my youth, God, you have taught me, and to this day I declare your marvellous deeds. Even when I am old and grey, do not forsake me, my God, till I declare your power to the next generation, your mighty acts to all who are to come.

Sometimes it takes us by surprise when we catch a glimpse of ourselves in a passing reflection in a shop window. Who is that grey-haired, slightly frail-looking older person? Whoever we are, these later years of life do find us. But God still has work for us.

The psalmist reminds us that God is with us, as he has been throughout our lives. He will not forsake us. In the present, we are encouraged to keep telling others about all God has done for us and for them. Then we are to tell the *next* generation – younger adults, grandchildren, neighbours – about God. Beyond this, the psalmist encourages us to keep thinking about the future – 'mighty acts to all who are to come' – and keep praying for God's work in our world in coming years.

Let's begin now by asking for God's help to tell others of his faithfulness to us over the years; to look for opportunities to talk about him with younger members of our families; to pray for the future of our troubled world as God works out his purposes.

■ PRAYER

Lord God, help me to find opportunities today to declare 'your marvellous deeds'. Amen

Luke 2:36–38 (NIV, abridged)

Faithful prayer

There was also a prophet, Anna… She was very old; she had lived with her husband seven years after her marriage, and then was a widow until she was eighty-four. She never left the temple but worshipped night and day, fasting and praying. Coming up to them… she gave thanks to God and spoke about the child to all who were looking forward to the redemption of Jerusalem.

Take a few moments to think about our world: troubled areas and wars; politics at home; people you know who are experiencing difficulties. Where in all this can you see God at work?

Anna, 84 years old, shows us faithful living. Despite hardship, she hasn't stopped worshipping God and praying. She is so alert to God's voice that she hears his prompting, pointing her to baby Jesus as he is brought to the temple with his parents. With prophetical insight, she recognises him as the long-awaited Messiah who would bring redemption to his people – and gives thanks for God's gift.

When we focus on God's plans and not just our own, we begin to see what he is doing in our world and in other people's lives. Think of your family, your community, the wider world. What might God be doing in these different situations? How might you work with him faithfully in your own life?

■ PRAYER

Lord, help me to notice what you are doing in the world and in the lives of others. Help me to work and pray faithfully that your will be done. Amen

Psalm 92:12–15 (NIV)

Fruitful living

The righteous will flourish like a palm tree, they will grow like a cedar of Lebanon; planted in the house of the Lord, they will flourish in the courts of our God. They will still bear fruit in old age, they will stay fresh and green, proclaiming, 'The Lord is upright; he is my Rock, and there is no wickedness in him.'

Fruitful? Flourishing? Fresh and green? It's easy to think that such ideas must only be for those with life ahead of them. But here the psalmist makes it clear that God sees and promises fruitfulness for those of us who are older too. You might have 'retired', you may not be as physically active as you once were, but God sees you as beautiful and strong as a 'cedar of Lebanon'.

Our western society may make us feel that older people can't contribute much. But here the psalmist brings a different perspective. In God's family, although as human beings we sometimes fail, potential is recognised and 'fruit' nurtured and delivered. Perhaps that's one way in which God's people are called to be different. Part of that fruitfulness is seen in our sustained trust and testimony in our God, our 'Rock'.

What is God calling you to be for him in whatever situation you find yourself now? What kind of fruit is he looking for in your life today? How might you flourish?

■ PRAYER

Thank you, Lord, that you are my rock. Help me to continue to flourish and to grow ever more fruitful as I serve you. Amen

Joel 2:28–29 (NIV)

I have a dream

'And afterwards, I will pour out my Spirit on all people. Your sons and daughters will prophesy, your old men will dream dreams, your young men will see visions. Even on my servants, both men and women, I will pour out my Spirit in those days.'

'I have a dream' – those famous words spoken by Martin Luther King in 1963 – echo those quoted here by the prophet Joel in the Bible, 'Your old men will dream dreams.' More than this, God promises that his Spirit will be poured out on all who are his servants. In Joel's time the words brought hope to a people terrified by their approaching enemies. At Pentecost, after the Spirit had come, the writer repeats them (Acts 2:17–18), applying them to current times. God lifts his people's eyes to future hope in him.

These verses reassure us that God works not only through the young, but older people as well. God isn't bothered by age or gender; his words are for those who are his 'servants'. Their dreams can bring hope to others. God pours out his Spirit on them, giving them strength and power to be his witnesses.

What hopes and dreams is God giving you for our world? How might you speak out God's encouragement for now and for the future?

■ PRAYER

Lord God, pour out your Spirit afresh on me so that I might be your witness to others today. Amen

Luke 2:26–30 (NIV, abridged)

Led by the Spirit

It had been revealed to [Simeon] by the Holy Spirit that he would not die before he had seen the Lord's Messiah. Moved by the Spirit, he went into the temple courts. When the parents brought in the child Jesus… Simeon took him in his arms and praised God, saying: 'Sovereign Lord, as you have promised… my eyes have seen your salvation.'

Imagine what a wonderful moment this must have been for Simeon. God had assured him that he would not die before he had seen 'the Lord's Messiah' who would bring light and salvation. At God's prompting he goes into the temple, sees the young baby and takes him in his arms. Immediately he knows who this is. Imagine the astonishment of his parents, and perhaps their relief, hearing that this elderly man – after the angels, shepherds and magi – sees the specialness of the child Jesus too.

Throughout his life, Simeon had been waiting for God's promises to be fulfilled. Always alert to the Spirit's leading, Simeon had not given up because he was old. So he followed God's prompting on that day… and received an astounding revelation as he looked at Jesus. Simeon, being in the right place at the right time, met God at a crucial moment: a crucial moment of revelation for us all.

■ PRAYER

What are you waiting for? Keep watching and praying. Listen out for the Spirit's leading in your life today.

Matthew 6:1a, 3–4 (NIV)

Giving to others

'Be careful not to practise your righteousness in front of others to be seen by them… When you give to the needy, do not let your left hand know what your right hand is doing, so that your giving may be in secret. Then your Father, who sees what is done in secret, will reward you.'

Just because we're older doesn't mean that we can't serve God. One way to do this might be through giving to others. We may not be rich in terms of money in the bank, but we are wealthy in other ways. Years of experience have given us wisdom as well as practical resources that could be of help to others.

I can remember times in earlier life when older Christians helped me with good practical advice, hospitality or financial support… and in other ways through which I have been blessed by God because of their willingness to give to me and my family. Maybe we feel we can no longer do much on the big stage of God's work, but what could we do quietly to help others in their living for him?

What we are able to give may not seem much (remember the widow's offering in Luke 21:1–4), but God sees, knows the cost for us and is pleased.

■ PRAYER

Lord, thank you for the resources you have given me. Help me to be ready to share these with others for the sake of your kingdom. Amen

Ephesians 6:18 (NIV)

Keep on praying

And pray in the Spirit on all occasions with all kinds of prayers and requests. With this in mind, be alert and always keep on praying for all the Lord's people.

One good thing about being older is having more time to pray. When I was younger, I remember being surprised and blessed to discover that older people were praying for me. When we're busy with careers, children and other activities it can be difficult to find the time and space we might like for prayer.

Now that life is less pressured, we may have more time to reflect on what is happening in the church, at home or in other parts of the world. We notice the struggles of our friends and family in clearer ways. Now, maybe, we can take regular time to let the Spirit lead us in our thinking about others, to be alert to their needs and pray for them. If night-time is not easy for you, with anxieties and worries crowding out sleep, why not deliberately pray for others in those moments?

Here is God's call to us: it's a significant way in which we can serve God. Let's join in with what he is doing in our world, the church and other people's lives as we pray.

■ **PRAYER**

Who or what will you pray for? Who is anxious and hurting? Do you know of Christians in other parts of the world who are suffering? Bring your prayers and requests to God now.

Psalm 78:4b, 6 (NIV)

Tell the next generation

We will tell the next generation the praiseworthy deeds of the Lord, his power and the wonders he has done... so that the next generation would know them, even the children yet to be born, and they in turn would tell their children.

Reflect for a moment on good things that have happened in your life because of God's generosity and love for you. Who could you tell? Maybe you have grandchildren, busy younger relatives; maybe you know young people in your church. The Lord has work for those of us who are older: 'tell the next generation the praiseworthy deeds of the Lord'.

As we talk with and live alongside younger people in the present, we are to encourage them to see how God has been at work in the past, is at work in their lives now and is already at work for future generations. Our words and actions in the present may bring news of God's love to those who are yet to be born.

I remember with thankfulness my mother-in-law. Into her late 80s she would go into local schools to take assemblies for the children who were about to move to secondary schools. Her words would assure them of God's love for them as they went forward in their lives. There may be different opportunities for us, but how could we tell the next generation?

■ PRAYER

Thank you, Lord, for how you are at work through generations. Help me to play my part in telling others today. Amen

Revelation 21:1a, 3–4a (NIV, abridged)

Hope for the future

Then I saw a new heaven and a new earth... And I heard a loud voice from the throne saying, 'Look! God's dwelling-place is now among people, and he will dwell with them. They will be his people, and God himself will be with them and be their God. He will wipe every tear from their eyes. There will be no more death or mourning or crying or pain.'

Sometimes it feels too difficult to watch the day's news on TV. 'Wars and rumours of wars' (Matthew 24:6) seem to threaten peace and safety around the world. Without faith there could be no hope for the future – or present. In these verses, the apostle John, having written at length about apocalyptic events, now speaks to those who put their trust in God. Whatever our personal circumstances, we need this encouragement too.

God will renew our world though we don't yet understand how. And God himself will be with his people. He will deal with heartache, pain and death. He will 'wipe every tear from their eyes'. This is a vision of life which lifts our eyes from the suffering and uncertainty of present times to a certain future of renewal, safety, healing and peace.

Think of those you know who have a special need of God's comfort and healing today. How might you help them to know God's comfort and discover this hope for the future?

■ PRAYER

Thank God for these words of promise. Ask him to help you share your hope in him with others you meet today.

The hope of glory

Angela Tilby

The writer and Christian apologist C.S. Lewis, author of the famous 'The Chronicles of Narnia' novels, once wrote a book called *The Weight of Glory*, in which he reflected on the meaning of the word 'glory' in the Bible. He argued that we would understand 'glory' better if we understood its Hebrew root.

'Glory' translates the word *kabod* which usually means 'density' or 'solidity'. Hence the 'weight' of glory.

When we attribute glory to God we are acknowledging that God is simply the source of all reality, the presence, power and fullness of all that is. As part of creation we are already connected to God. Our uniqueness as human beings is that we have the chance to recognise this and realise it in the way we live, work and pray.

Our readings about glory focus on the hope and loss of glory in the Old Testament and the glory of God in Christ manifested in his birth, death and resurrection. Part of the gift that comes with getting older is that we can become more sensitive to the glory around us and within us, and more receptive to the glory God has prepared for us.

Revelation 5:11–12 (NRSV)

Worthy of glory

Then I looked, and I heard the voice of many angels surrounding the throne and the living creatures and the elders; they numbered myriads of myriads and thousands of thousands, singing with full voice, 'Worthy is the Lamb that was slaughtered to receive power and wealth and wisdom and might and honour and glory and blessing!'

Getting older can be a lonely time. Even with faith, optimism, health and good friends, our horizons can seem to get smaller, as we come reluctantly to realise that our physical and mental capacities are not what they once were.

Much present-day advice on ageing well reminds us of the importance of staying connected, and for Christians our most important connection is with God, revealed as he is in Jesus Christ. Today's passage offers us a window into heaven, which is seen here as a place of company and rejoicing. This is what lies ahead, and we can see that there is much more going on in the heavenly realms than we can ever realise or experience within the limits of earthly existence. In the Christian life we are always moving on; those countless myriads beyond us are not only before us but around us now, supporting our daily pilgrimage.

■ **PRAYER**

Glory to God in the highest! Lord of lords and King of kings, give courage and cheerfulness to your people on earth and the gift of hope on every step of our journey, today and always. Amen

Psalm 24:9–10 (NRSV)

The king of glory

Lift up your heads, O gates! and be lifted up, O ancient doors, that the King of glory may come in! Who is this King of glory? The Lord of hosts, he is the King of glory.

The image in this psalm is of the Jewish temple in Jerusalem. Streams of pilgrims and visitors have climbed the rocky path to Mount Zion and now await the start of an annual festival, a joyful event which celebrates the Lord's kingship over all creation. It also looks forward to the earthly rule of God's anointed king.

So on one level this psalm celebrates King David and his successors, while on another it looks forward to the coming Son of David, the long hoped for, long expected Messiah. In the gospels this theme is played out in a different key. When 'great David's greater Son' enters Jerusalem in triumph it is Palm Sunday. He rides a humble donkey. Later he will cleanse the temple and incur the wrath of the religious rulers.

We begin to discover that the weight of glory is also the weight of challenge and the start of the suffering which will bring us salvation. Yet the one who comes is still the same Lord, the one who can be trusted, whose promises and mercy are rock solid.

■ PRAYER

Open the doors of my heart, good Lord, to receive you this day. Come in your glory, come in your power, come with healing and forgiveness and make us whole. Amen

1 Samuel 4:21a (NRSV)

Glory lost and found

She named the child Ichabod, meaning, 'The glory has departed from Israel,' because the ark of God had been captured.

The birth of a baby is usually a cause for joy, but poor Ichabod's birth coincided with the capture of the Ark of God's presence from the Israelite shrine at Shiloh and the death of the child's father and grandfather. His mother mourns both for her personal loss and for the loss of the most precious symbol of God's presence with his people.

There are times in all of our lives when we sense 'the glory has departed', when the presence of God and the blessings of life are overwhelmed by loss and sorrow. At this time of year and as we grow older, we should try to remember that exile and loss, seen through the eyes of faith, always point to restoration and renewal. The glory may have departed for now, but the promise is of return. As the ancient hymn puts it, 'From glory to glory advancing, we praise thee, O Lord.'

■ PRAYER

Hear our prayer, Lord, when the clouds of loss overwhelm us and we lose the vision of your glory. Help us to trust that your face will shine upon us once again and that we may know you as our Saviour, Lord and God. Amen

Isaiah 40:4–5 (NRSV)

Glory revealed

Every valley shall be lifted up, and every mountain and hill be made low; the uneven ground shall become level, and the rough places a plain. Then the glory of the Lord shall be revealed, and all flesh shall see it together, for the mouth of the Lord has spoken.

For those who know and love Handel's 'Messiah' it is hard to read those words without being reminded of the joyful aria and chorus which he composed as a setting for them. Isaiah is ministering to God's people in exile. Here he prophesies that, just as the Red Sea rolled back to allow God's people to escape from Egypt, so a highway will appear where once there were mountains and valleys, to make plain the way of the Lord, to reveal his glory and enable their return.

The good news of Advent is news of liberation, of release, of the end of captivity. We may think our current obstacles are insurmountable, but God's glory can still break through, even through our particular circumstances and our natural limitations. What are the deep valleys you need help to cross today, and what mountains lie in your path?

■ PRAYER

Lord of glory, shine upon me this day. Speak to me tenderly of your love. Support me in my trials. Come to me as I wait expectantly for you, for you are the hope of nations and peoples, you are the king of glory. Amen

Ezekiel 43:1–2, 4–5 (NRSV)

Glory restored

Then he brought me to the gate, the gate facing east. And there the glory of the God of Israel was coming from the east; the sound was like the sound of mighty waters, and the earth shone with his glory… As the glory of the Lord entered the temple by the gate facing east, the spirit lifted me up and brought me into the inner court, and the glory of the Lord filled the temple.

The prophet Ezekiel was sent to care for God's people when they were deported from the Holy Land to Babylon. He lived among them through their exile, which he interpreted as punishment for their unfaithfulness, while also encouraging them to hope for God's forgiveness.

Throughout his ministry he had been conscious of God's presence, even in the alien territory to which he had been sent. Now he has a vision of the return of God's glory to the temple in Jerusalem. This prophecy took a long time to come to fruition. The exiles who eventually returned found the temple wrecked. It took enormous effort and courage to rebuild it and to restore its glory. But what Ezekiel's vision gave to the exiles was the encouragement they needed to endure their present suffering, knowing that God had a future for them when all losses would be restored.

■ PRAYER

Lord, may I catch a glimpse of your glory this day and so be encouraged to face all that lies ahead. Amen

Luke 2:8–10 (NRSV)

Surrounded by glory

Now in that same region there were shepherds living in the fields, keeping watch over their flock by night. Then an angel of the Lord stood before them, and the glory of the Lord shone around them, and they were terrified. But the angel said to them, 'Do not be afraid, for see, I am bringing you good news of great joy to all the people.'

According to the Bible, one of the most natural human reactions to an angelic visitation is terror. We simply do not expect the boundaries between earth and heaven to be lifted, for the glory which surrounds us all the time to suddenly be revealed to our mortal senses.

But holy terror is a prelude to blessing. The glory breaks through, the holy birth is announced, the song of the angels gives the shepherds courage to make the journey to Bethlehem. What holds us up in our Christian lives is not holy terror, but the anxiety which we produce from our own fears and fantasies. Anxiety is very common whether we are young or old, and it is something we have to learn to deal with. Prayer could be one way of helping us leave our daily worries with God and to trust him more deeply both in the present moment and for the future.

■ PRAYER

Lord, may the song of the angels break in upon us, giving us the vision and courage to rise above our daily preoccupations and seek you in unexpected places. Amen

John 1:14, 16 (NRSV)

The glory of the Son

And the Word became flesh and lived among us, and we have seen his glory, the glory as of a father's only son, full of grace and truth... From his fullness we have all received, grace upon grace.

'Grace upon grace' is a wonderful phrase to ponder. We can trust God because both scripture and human experience point to his endless grace, his mercy. The true meaning of the incarnation, the faith summed up in the creeds, is that God loved us so much that he came in Christ to share his divine life with us. 'From his fullness we have all received.'

The gospels give us many examples of Jesus bringing joy and hope to those who encountered him. He still rejoices in our company and brings us peace, restoring the potential for love that we have lost through the inherited sins of humanity and our own personal failings. There is so much to give thanks for. Today, try to remind yourself of God's goodness. Counting your blessings is good spiritual practice, and an antidote to those bitter regrets which can accumulate with advancing age. God's mercies are new every morning.

■ PRAYER

O blessed, incarnate Lord, glory to you in your sacred humanity, praise to you in your loving divinity. Lead me step by step to follow you, that I may cry with all the angels: 'Blessing and glory and wisdom and thanksgiving and honour and power and might be to our God forever and ever!' (Revelation 7:12). Amen

John 2:9–11 (NRSV)

Signs of glory

When the person in charge tasted the water that had become wine and did not know where it came from (though the servants who had drawn the water knew), the person called the bridegroom and said to him, 'Everyone serves the good wine first and then the inferior wine after the guests have become drunk. But you have kept the good wine until now.' Jesus did this, the first of his signs, in Cana of Galilee, and revealed his glory, and his disciples believed in him.

If anyone doubted that God rejoices in humanity, this story of the wedding of Cana should put us right. This is the first of what John calls Jesus' 'signs' and it reveals his glory by showing us who he is. He is the promised Saviour who comes from the glory of God and rejoices in human nature. He is at home among the guests at a marriage feast, and he provides more than enough wine for the party to go on when the supplies have run out.

Today, think of the great celebrations of your life, when you have felt truly blessed and overflowing with joy and gratitude. Picture Jesus among the guests and express your thanks to him.

■ PRAYER

Lord, you give me so much. Give me one thing more: a humble, loving and truly grateful heart, always alert to your promptings, penitent for my failings, aware of your mercies and hopeful for the fulfilment of all your promises. Amen

2 Corinthians 3:17–18 (NRSV)

Look towards the glory

Now the Lord is the Spirit, and where the Spirit of the Lord is, there is freedom. And all of us, with unveiled faces, seeing the glory of the Lord as though reflected in a mirror, are being transformed into the same image from one degree of glory to another, for this comes from the Lord, the Spirit.

It is a rule of life that we become what we attend to. If we pay constant attention to our grievances then we become more aggrieved not less, until our whole being is taken over by complaint. The Christian alternative is to look away from ourselves and our preoccupations. Gratitude is the seed of Christian freedom, that freedom which the Spirit gives.

We enter this freedom by developing an attitude of wonder, in simple thankfulness for God's provision for us, in fostering friendship with our neighbours and being ready to forgive. An attitude of gratitude is always transformative. And this transformation is not only for ourselves. If we are looking towards the glory we ourselves will shine, and others will see glory in us. That once popular worship song, 'Shine, Jesus, shine', suggested that the glory of Jesus could reflect in our faces. Transformation is an ongoing process. Gratitude not only sets us free, it prepares us for the life of heaven.

■ PRAYER

Lord, lead us step by step, into the glorious liberty you desire for your children, which is revealed in the face of Jesus Christ our Lord. Amen

Ephesians 1:17–20 (NRSV)

An education in hope

I pray that the God of our Lord Jesus Christ, the Father of glory, may give you a spirit of wisdom and revelation as you come to know him, so that, with the eyes of your heart enlightened, you may perceive what is the hope to which he has called you, what are the riches of his glorious inheritance among the saints, and what is the immeasurable greatness of his power for us who believe, according to the workings of his great power. God put this power to work in Christ when he raised him from the dead and seated him at his right hand in the heavenly places.

The Christian life is an education in hope, a reminder that there are no permanent stopping places on our Christian pilgrimage. There are always new promises, new perspectives, new discoveries. Christianity may not always be accompanied by optimism, but it must be accompanied by hope.

This is summed up beautifully in a parallel verse, Colossians 1:27, 'Christ in you, the hope of glory.' As we come to recognise God's mercy in Christ, who is both human and divine, so the gift of hope is born in us and we begin to participate in the fruits of Christ's resurrection.

■ PRAYER

Christ, my way, my truth, my life; keep my eyes fixed on you, so that at the end of my earthly pilgrimage I can acknowledge with a joyful heart that you are my Lord and my God. Amen

Everything has its time

For everything there is a season, and a time for every matter under heaven.

ECCLESIASTES 3:1 (NRSV)

These four months seem to cover many seasons, as we start back after the summer break and move from harvest to autumn, Advent and Christmas, and at BRF Ministries we produce resources from all our ministry teams for all these seasons in turn.

Our resources include books, greetings cards, podcasts, a wide range of training opportunities, Facebook Live sessions, the occasional webinar, and meet-ups, both in person and online. They focus on Anna Chaplaincy, Living Faith, Messy Church and Parenting for Faith, but at the heart we are all BRF Ministries, playing our part in our mission to inspire people of all ages to grow in Christian faith.

To find out about all of the exciting things we are doing, visit our website **brf.org.uk**. From there you can find out about us as a charity and follow links to the ministry websites, and the big red buttons at the top of the page take you straight to our web store and our donations page.

In order to produce these resources and events we are entirely dependent on donations from individuals, churches, charitable trusts and gifts in wills. Every donation is important to us and we are deeply grateful for your continued generosity. If you would like to support us now and in the future, you can become a Friend of BRF Ministries by making a monthly gift of £2 or more – we thank you for your friendship.

Find out more at **brf.org.uk/donate** or get in touch with us on **01235 462305** or via **giving@brf.org.uk**.

The fundraising team at BRF Ministries

The lectionary readings for Advent speak of making a straight path towards God, but many of us find our own route decidedly winding. Biblical characters in the story of the incarnation are called to set out on the road to discipleship using any means of carriage they can. This book offers user-friendly encouragement (with the occasional spur onwards) to explore what helps and what hinders us in this journey to deeper encounter with the flesh and blood God whom we find in scripture, in our lived experience and in the least of his sisters and brothers.

Donkey Roads and Camel Treks
A pilgrim's guide for Advent
Gemma Simmonds
978 0 80039 347 9 £9.99
brfonline.org.uk

Mindfulness is not new, and God's people down the centuries have always been encouraged to practise 'the sacrament of the present moment' – that is, to notice God in the events of everyday life and become attentive to that presence. Tony Horsfall explores six Bible stories that describe individuals encountering God, showing how we can learn how to notice the presence of the divine for ourselves. He also unpacks key spiritual practices that anyone can follow, and introduces insights from influential writers on the awareness of God in the ordinary.

Attentive to God
Being aware of God's presence in daily life
Tony Horsfall
978 1 80039 401 8 £9.99
brfonline.org.uk

To order

Online: **brfonline.org.uk**
Telephone: +44 (0)1865 319700
Mon–Fri 9.30–17.00
Post: complete this form and send to the address below

Delivery times within the UK are normally 15 working days. Prices are correct at the time of going to press but may change without prior notice.

BRF

Title	Issue	Price	Qty	Total
Donkey Roads and Camel Treks		£9.99		
Attentive to God		£9.99		
Bible Reflections for Older People (single copy)	Sep–Dec 2025	£5.75		
Bible Reflections for Older People (single copy)	Jan–Apr 2026	£5.75		

POSTAGE AND PACKING CHARGES			
Order value	UK	Europe	Rest of world
Under £7.00	£2.00	Available on request	Available on request
£7.00–£29.99	£3.00		
£30.00 and over	FREE		

*Please complete the Gift Aid declaration below

Total value of books	
Donation*	
Postage and packing	
Total for this order	

Please complete in BLOCK CAPITALS

Title .... First name/initials .... Surname ....

Address ....

.... Postcode ....

Acc. No. .... Telephone ....

Email ....

Method of payment

❑ Cheque (made payable to BRF) ❑ MasterCard / Visa

Card no. ☐☐☐☐ ☐☐☐☐ ☐☐☐☐ ☐☐☐☐

Expires end M M Y Y Security code ☐☐☐ Last 3 digits on the reverse of the card

BRF Ministries Gift Aid Declaration

giftaid it

In order to Gift Aid your donations, you must tick the box below.

❑ I want to Gift Aid my donation and any donation I make in the future or have made in the past four years to BRF Ministries.

I am a UK taxpayer and understand that if I pay less Income Tax and/or Capital Gains Tax in the current tax year than the amount of Gift Aid claimed on all my donations, it is my responsibility to pay any difference. Please notify BRF Ministries if you want to cancel this declaration, change your name or home address, or no longer pay sufficient tax on your income and/or capital gains.

Please return this form to:
BRF Ministries, 15 The Chambers, Vineyard, Abingdon OX14 3FE | **enquiries@brf.org.uk**
For terms and cancellation information, please visit brfonline.org.uk/terms.

We will use your personal data to process this order. From time to time we may send you information about the work of BRF Ministries. Please contact us if you wish to discuss your mailing preferences **brf.org.uk/privacy**

Registered with FUNDRAISING REGULATOR

BROP0325

BIBLE REFLECTIONS FOR OLDER PEOPLE **GROUP SUBSCRIPTION FORM**

All our Bible reading notes can be ordered online
by visiting **brfonline.org.uk/subscriptions**

The group subscription rate for ***Bible Reflections for Older People*** will be £17.25 per person until April 2026.

☐ I would like to take out a group subscription for .... (*quantity*) copies.

☐ Please start my order with the January 2026 / May 2026 / September 2026* issue.
(**delete as appropriate*)

Please do not send any money with your order. Send your order to BRF Ministries and we will send you an invoice.

Name and address of the person organising the group subscription:

Title .... First name/initials .... Surname ....

Address ....

.... Postcode ....

Telephone .... Email ....

Church ....

Name and address of the person paying the invoice if the invoice needs to be sent directly to them:

Title .... First name/initials .... Surname ....

Address ....

.... Postcode ....

Telephone .... Email ....

Please return this form to:
BRF Ministries, 15 The Chambers, Vineyard, Abingdon OX14 3FE | **enquiries@brf.org.uk**
For terms and cancellation information, please visit brfonline.org.uk/terms.

Bible Reading Fellowship is a charity (233280) and company limited by guarantee (301324), registered in England and Wales

BROP0325

BIBLE REFLECTIONS FOR OLDER PEOPLE **INDIVIDUAL/GIFT SUBSCRIPTION FORM**

To order online or set up a recurring subscription,
visit **brfonline.org.uk/bible-reflections-for-older-people**

☐ I would like to take out a subscription (*complete your name and address details only once*)
☐ I would like to give a gift subscription (*please provide both names and addresses*)

Title .... First name/initials .... Surname ....

Address ....

.... Postcode ....

Telephone .... Email ....

Gift subscription name ....

Gift subscription address ....

.... Postcode ....

Gift message (*20 words max. or include your own gift card*):

....

....

Please send ***Bible Reflections for Older People*** beginning with the January 2026 / May 2026 / September 2026* issue (**delete as appropriate*):

(*please tick box*)	**UK**	**Europe**	**Rest of world**
Bible Reflections for Older People	☐ £22.80	☐ £30.75	☐ £37.05

Total enclosed £ .... (*cheques should be made payable to 'BRF'*)

Please charge my MasterCard / Visa with £ ....

Card no. ☐☐☐☐ ☐☐☐☐ ☐☐☐☐ ☐☐☐☐

Expires end ☐☐ ☐☐ (M M Y Y) Security code ☐☐☐ Last 3 digits on the reverse of the card

We will use your personal data to process this order. From time to time we may send you information about the work of BRF Ministries. Please contact us if you wish to discuss your mailing preferences **brf.org.uk/privacy.**

Please return this form to:

BRF Ministries, 15 The Chambers, Vineyard, Abingdon OX14 3FE | **enquiries@brf.org.uk**
For terms and cancellation information, please visit brfonline.org.uk/terms.

Bible Reading Fellowship is a charity (233280) and company limited by guarantee (301324), registered in England and Wales

BROP0325